STORAGE

A DISCARDED

DO NOT REMOVE
CARDS FROM POCKET

ALLEN COUNTY PUBLIC LIBRARY

FORT WAYNE, INDIANA 46802

You may return this book to any agency, branch,
or bookmobile of the Allen County Public Library.

DEMCO

the LAWRENCE TAYLOR story

Howard Liss

ENSLOW PUBLISHERS, INC.

Bloy St. & Ramsey Ave.   P.O. Box 38
Box 777   Aldershot
Hillside, N.J. 07205   Hants GU12 6BP
U.S.A.   U.K.

Copyright © 1987 by Howard Liss

Library of Congress Cataloging in Publication Data

Liss, Howard.
   The Lawrence Taylor story.

   Includes index.
   Summary: A biography, emphasizing the career, of the star linebacker of the New York Giants football team.
   1. Taylor, Lawrence, 1959-   —Juvenile literature.
2. Football players—United States—Biography—Juvenile literature. 3. New York Giants (Football team)—Juvenile literature. [1. Taylor, Lawrence, 1959-   . 2. Football players. 3. Afro-Americans—Biography]
I. Title.
GV939.T34L57 1987 796.332'092'4 [B] [92] 86-19856
ISBN 0-89490-136-2

Printed in the U.S.A.

10 9 8 7 6 5 4 3 2 1

Illustration Credits

Jerry Pinkus, pp. 9, 22, 24, 27, 29, 31, 32, 34, 37, 39, 40, 42, 43, 46, 48, 51, 52, 55, 57, front cover; University of North Carolina, p. 16.

CONTENTS

7128493

For Nicholas Dorans—a new football fan.

North Carolina was leading Texas Tech. The score was 9–3. But Tech was driving toward North Carolina's goal and had the football on North Carolina's 5-yard line. A touchdown would tie the score. The point after touchdown would put Tech in the lead.

The teams lined up. The Tech quarterback got the ball from the center. He began to drop back for a pass.

Suddenly, a huge player wearing a North Carolina jersey came rushing in. He got to the quarterback and knocked him down. The Tech quarterback was hit so hard that he fumbled. Carolina recovered and went on to win the game.

Later that season, North Carolina was playing Clemson. The Clemson team was losing, 24–19, but they were marching ahead toward the Carolina goal. There wasn't much time left to play. Clemson had no more time-outs, but they seemed certain to score a touchdown and go ahead of North Carolina.

The Clemson quarterback went back to pass. Again, a big player wearing a North Carolina jersey cracked through the line. He banged into the Clemson quarterback and knocked him off his feet. Before Clemson could get back and try again, the game was over. North Carolina had won.

The big man who knocked over both the Texas Tech quarterback and the Clemson quarterback was Lawrence Taylor, the North Carolina Tar Heels' great linebacker.

When the 1980 college football season ended, Lawrence Taylor was named to the All-American team. That meant he was one of the best football players in the country.

Taylor—everybody called him "L.T."—stood 6 feet 3 inches tall. He weighed 243 pounds. For a man that size he was unusually fast. He could run faster than most other linebackers. And he was quick.

In football, fast is not really the same as quick. Fast simply means running straight ahead in a race and beating other runners. L.T. could do that.

Quick means taking only one or two steps and then running at top speed. Quick means changing direction in the twinkling of an eye. Quick means starting to move just a split second ahead of other players. Lawrence Taylor was *very* quick. There was no doubt that he would be drafted by a pro football team.

There are rules in a pro draft. The team with the worst record gets first pick of the best college players.

The team with the next poorest record gets second choice. Finally, the team that has won the Super Bowl game picks last.

In 1980, the New Orleans Saints had the worst record in pro football. The team had won only one game and lost fifteen games. The second pick would belong to the New York Giants. They had won four and lost twelve.

Most sportswriters said the Saints would choose George Rogers as their first pick. Rogers was a very fine running back who had played at the University of South Carolina.

Most sportswriters also said that the Giants would pick Lawrence Taylor.

In a way that was a strange choice. The Giants already had some good linebackers, such as Harry Carson, Brad Van Pelt, and Brian Kelley. But the Giants wanted Taylor, too. The coaches were sure he would become a great pro star.

L.T. liked the idea of playing for the Giants. There were many opportunities for athletes in big cities. If he made good with the Giants, he might be signed for television commercials. Probably he would get a good job after his playing days were over. The future looked bright for Taylor.

As a rule, athletes do not talk about a contract with the owners of a pro team. They hire agents to do that. It is the agent's job to get as much money as he can for the athlete. Mike Trope, Taylor's agent, demanded a lot of money to sign L.T. The newspapers reported that Taylor wanted $375,000 to play for three years.

It was also reported that some players on the Giants were upset by that news. Carson, Van Pelt, and Kelley had been playing with the Giants for years, but they did not get that much money. There was a rumor that they might walk off the team.

L.T. was puzzled. He did not understand why other players should be jealous of him. All pro athletes want a lot of money. Sometimes they get the money, sometimes they don't. But if L.T. was paid well, sooner or later the others would also get more money. Besides, there was so much L.T. wanted to do.

"I'm going to buy my family a big house," he said. "My mom and dad have worked a long time. They deserve the best. I want to repay them for all they did for me and my brothers."

Still, L.T. did not want to play with unhappy teammates. He sent a telegram to the Giants, asking them not to draft him.

Suddenly, everything seemed to be going wrong for L.T. Steve Streater, his best friend and teammate in college, was hurt in an automobile accident. His car had skidded in a rainstorm and crashed. Streater was paralyzed.

L.T. was in New York when he heard the news. He rushed to the hospital to be with his friend. He talked to Steve and tried to comfort him. Streater would surely have been drafted by a pro team. Now that dream was ended.

"Steve's accident really hit me hard," L.T. said. "He was an outstanding player. And he's such a wonderful

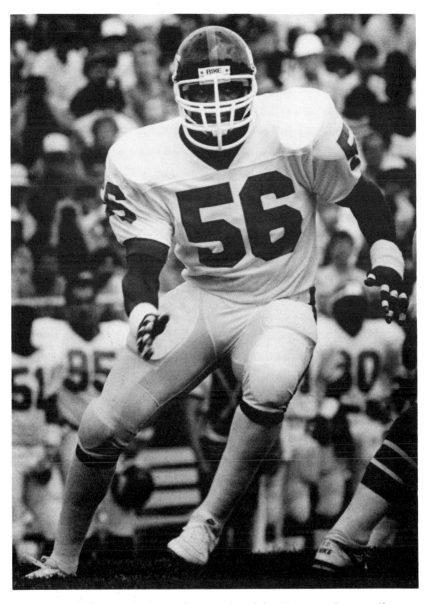

Lawrence Taylor is both fast and quick. He can change direction in the twinkling of an eye.

human being. I am dedicating my first pro season to my buddy, Steve Streater."

When L.T. returned to New York, he learned that the other Giants were not really angry with him. They did not care how much money he got, as long as they got more money, too. L.T. understood how they felt. In pro football, the average player lasts only about four or five years. He might get hurt seriously and be forced to quit. Or someone else might come along, a player who is bigger, stronger, and faster. Then the veteran player loses his job.

Big L.T. signed a contract with the Giants. Then the sportswriters began to tease him. They wrote that Taylor liked to play video games. One of his favorite TV shows was *The Three Stooges*.

Taylor just chuckled. "That's true," he said. "I like video games. A lot of people enjoy video games. And I think The Three Stooges are funny. Lots of folks laugh at them."

Now it was time for summer training camp. "I'm looking forward to it," L.T. said. "I know I've got a lot to learn."

Oh, yes, L.T. did buy his parents a new home. It was the nicest and biggest house on the block.

Lawrence Taylor was born on February 4, 1959, in Williamsburg, Virginia. His parents had three sons. Lawrence was the one in the middle. His dad, Clarence Taylor, Jr., drove a truck at the Newport News shipyards.

Mr. Taylor worked hard, but he always had time to play with his sons. Little Lawrence would chase his father around the small yard. He would grab his dad's leg and hold on. Then he would look up at his father's smiling face.

"I got you that time, Dad." Then he would laugh.

Iris Taylor, L.T.'s mother, began giving her children lessons even before they started school. The TV set was turned off. She taught the boys numbers, shapes, and sizes. Lawrence learned quickly, but he didn't like anyone to teach him. He had to figure things out for himself.

Lawrence was the same kind of student in school. He didn't study. He would get a C or a D in most of his subjects. Mrs. Taylor wanted him to study, but he wouldn't.

However, young Lawrence did have some good ideas of his own. For example, one day he asked his mother to lend him two dollars.

"Why do you want the money?" Mrs. Taylor asked.

"I'm going to buy candy," said the boy.

"That's silly," said Mrs. Taylor. "You shouldn't eat so much candy."

"It's not for me," Lawrence explained. "I'm going to sell the candy to the students in my school."

The next day he paid his mother back the two dollars she had loaned him. He had also made two dollars profit. He had sold most of the candy at lunchtime.

Lawrence always enjoyed sports. His favorite game was baseball. He was a catcher and one of the best batters on the Lafayette High team.

Lawrence also enjoyed basketball and sometimes played football. But he didn't play for Lafayette High at first. He joined a team in the city league but it wasn't a very good team. When a player came out of the game for a while, he would smoke a cigarette.

Perhaps Lawrence didn't care for football then because he wasn't big or strong. Some of his friends thought he could become a good football player, but at first Lawrence didn't want to join the Lafayette team.

12

It was L.T.'s baseball coach who made him try out for the football team. He said to Lawrence, "You had better work hard at baseball. You will never become a good football player." L.T. wanted to prove his baseball coach was wrong, and he joined the football team.

He was a junior in high school at that time. For a while it seemed that his baseball coach was right. Other players just pushed him away. Blockers would knock him down easily. He would run all over the field. When the play was over, he would be in the wrong place.

L.T. made a lot of mistakes in the first few games. But he was learning from those mistakes. Then Lafayette played Bethel High School. That was when L.T. showed what he could do.

He came rushing in at the Bethel quarterback. When the quarterback threw a pass, L.T. leaped high. His fingers tipped the ball up into the air. He caught the ball and ran for a touchdown.

L.T. kept improving. Perhaps he was lucky, or maybe he just seemed to know where the football would be. He made a lot of good plays. Sometimes he would tackle a runner on the other side of the field. He wasn't supposed to be there, but he seemed to come just in time.

Now Lawrence liked football better than any other sport. He made up his mind to be a great player and worked hard. That summer, between his junior and senior years, he began to grow. In a few months he was almost four inches taller. He gained about twenty pounds.

L.T. was a star in his last year in high school. He would come busting out of the line and smack into the players on other teams. He had a lot of confidence in himself. His teammates said that L.T. was better than most high school players they had seen.

Lawrence had a lot of friends in high school. He and a few other boys formed a kind of club. They called themselves "D'Fellas." The group never got into serious trouble, but they did some things people should not do. They would drive very fast through the streets of Williamsburg. Or they would stay up all night, sitting near a railroad bridge, singing songs and drinking beer.

L.T. has always kept in touch with D'Fellas. They often visit each other. Sometimes he will go to Williamsburg for a while. Or else some of them will come to his house in New Jersey. They still enjoy playing cards together.

After high school, L.T. wanted to play college football. He needed an athletic scholarship. But not many colleges were interested in him. He had two good offers: one from the University of Richmond, the other from the University of North Carolina. He chose Carolina.

Unfortunately, some of L.T.'s bad habits did not change when he enrolled in college. He didn't care about studying. He would cut classes so that he could shoot a game of pool. Some people said he was a hoodlum. If somebody got in his way, he would just push that person aside. To L.T. everything was a joke. He got into fights and laughed about them.

Then, one day he met a girl named Linda. She later became his wife. But at first she didn't like L.T.

"Why do you always pick on people?" she said angrily. "Why do you push them around? You're so much bigger than they are."

No girl had ever talked that way to L.T. He liked Linda right away. He stopped going out much. Instead, he would sit in his room, hoping Linda would call him.

L.T. didn't push players around on the football field in his freshman year. Though he was still fast and quick, he began to lose confidence in himself. He didn't always know what was happening on the field. He made mistakes.

Some of the same things happened in his sophomore year. He played linebacker and also played in the line. He was discouraged from time to time. He thought that maybe he wasn't good enough after all. Yet he also knew that if he wasn't a good player, the coaches wouldn't let him play at all.

In his junior year, everything seemed to turn out right. He became the regular outside linebacker on the team. Outside and inside linebackers have different responsibilities. Inside linebackers must guard against running plays that go into the middle of the line and have to stop short passes over the middle. The outside linebackers must try to prevent end runs and must be ready for the short pass to the sideline. Because L.T. was so fast, he could often catch the ball carrier trying to run around end.

The North Carolina Tar Heels got off to a good start in 1979. They won their first four games, defeating South Carolina, Pittsburgh, Army, and Cincinnati. They lost to Wake Forest, 24–19.

L.T. practicing at the University of North Carolina.

The rest of the season was disappointing for the Tar Heels. They beat North Carolina State, but then they were tied by East Carolina. After that they lost two in a row, to Maryland and Clemson. However, North Carolina closed the season by defeating Virginia, 13–7, and the team was invited to play Michigan in the Gator Bowl.

In every game he played, L.T. seemed to get better and better. He was becoming one of the best outside linebackers in college football. He made hard tackles. He knocked over blockers who were trying to stop him. When a quarterback saw L.T. coming at him, he got rid of the ball immediately.

Perhaps L.T. did not "sack" the quarterback (tackle him behind the line of scrimmage). But he did make the passer throw the ball away, almost anyplace. That is called "putting pressure on the passer." The quarterback must throw the ball away or risk being tackled for a loss.

L.T. played a marvelous game against Michigan. He helped his team beat the Wolverines, 17–15. One play L.T. made practically finished Michigan. Lawrence went right at the quarterback, John Wangler. He sacked him for an 11-yard loss. L.T. tackled Wangler so hard that he had to leave the game.

In 1980, North Carolina was picked to be one of the top ten teams in the country. The Tar Heels proved how good they were in the first game. They beat Furman, 35–13. Then they defeated Texas Tech, 9–3. That was followed by a 17–3 victory over Maryland.

In the Maryland game, L.T. was a standout. He sacked the quarterback twice. He caught the ball carrier behind the line of scrimmage and tackled him for a loss. He recovered a fumble. Then he made eight more "solo" tackles. Frequently, a defensive player has help from a teammate when he tackles the ball carrier. A solo tackle means the defensive player makes the play by himself.

North Carolina continued its march against Georgia Tech. by winning that game, 33–0. In the third quarter, L.T. tackled the passer in his own end zone for a 2-point safety.

Wake Forest fell to the Tar Heels, 27–9. In that game, Wake Forest had the ball on the Carolina 20-yard line. On third down, L.T. banged through the line and sacked the quarterback for a 7-yard loss. Wake Forest had to settle for a field goal instead of a touchdown. Wake Forest did score a touchdown with only seconds left to play. By that time the Tar Heels had their substitutes on the field. L.T. and the first-string defense relaxed on the bench.

Next, the Tar Heels defeated North Carolina State, 28–8. In that game, L.T.'s friend, Steve Streater, showed how good he was. Streater was the team's safety man and punter. On fourth down, Steve faked a kick, kept the ball, and ran for a touchdown.

In all these victories, L.T. was "double-teamed." That meant the other team used two blockers to try and stop his charge. Often double-teaming didn't work. L.T. managed to find a way to get through. In the game against Oklahoma, L.T. was *triple-teamed*. That slowed Taylor. The Sooners drubbed the Tar Heels, 41–7.

North Carolina got back on the winning track against Clemson. It was a hard-fought game. The Tar Heels' defense was outstanding. In the fourth quarter, the Carolina line and linebackers actually pushed Clemson back 27 yards. First, tackle Donnell Thompson sacked the quarterback. Then it was L.T.'s turn to sack the quarterback.

Clemson had to punt, but they got a lucky break. The bouncing football touched a Carolina player, and Clemson recovered. They marched down the field. Clemson got to the Carolina 1-yard line. It was first down, goal to go.

Twice, Clemson's ball carrier tried to get into the end zone. Twice he was stopped by the Carolina defense. On third down, Clemson tried a pass. L.T. came racing in. He got through the blockers and sacked the quarterback for a loss. On fourth down Clemson tried another pass. It didn't connect. North Carolina held on to win the game, 24–19.

L.T. and his teammates won the rest of their games. They beat Virginia and Duke. The Tar Heels finished the season with a record of ten victories and only one loss. They were the champions of the Atlantic Coast Conference.

That year North Carolina went to the Bluebonnet Bowl. They played the University of Texas. The Tar Heels defeated the Longhorns, 16–7. L.T. was a demon on the field. He made seven solo tackles and helped out on another. He knocked down two passes.

But the award for Most Valuable Defensive Player of the game went to Steve Streater. Steve was just great.

He intercepted one pass, which led to a Carolina touchdown. He recovered a fumble. He knocked away two passes.

L.T. was happy for his friend. He said, "If I couldn't win the award, I'm glad Steve did. He is truly a fine football player."

Steve Streater was also named All-Conference safetyman and punter. The Washington Redskins wanted him to play on their team, but that was not to be.

For Lawrence Taylor, the 1980 season had been terrific. He had tackled a ball carrier behind the line of scrimmage twenty-two times. He had sacked the quarterback sixteen times.

The totals for his college career were amazing. In four years they added up to 192 tackles and 21 sacks of opposing quarterbacks. He had three interceptions and recovered three fumbles. He forced ten more fumbles. L.T. was easily the best linebacker in college ball.

After the Bluebonnet Bowl, L.T. was selected to play in the East-Wast Shrine Game and the Japan Bowl. Then, at last, his college playing days were finished. Although he didn't graduate, he was ready to play pro football.

Summer training camp was about to begin. Lawrence Taylor was interviewed by the New York sportswriters. He joked with them.

"I like to hit the guys playing against me," he said. "I like to eat quarterbacks." The sportswriters laughed. All defensive linemen and linebackers said things like that. L.T. still had to prove he could play pro football.

Rookies reported to training camp first. For them training lasted five weeks. The veterans had only four weeks of training. The old-timers knew what to expect, the rookies didn't.

The routine was the same every day except Sunday. The players were awakened at seven o'clock in the morning. Some players ate breakfast; others did not. Then practice began. It lasted from nine o'clock to

Lifting weights is an important part of training camp. Here L.T. shows how it is done.

eleven o'clock. After that the players rested. They had lunch. Perhaps they watched TV or took a nap. There was more practice from three o'clock to five o'clock in the afternoon. When practice was over, the players took showers. They had dinner. In the evenings there were squad meetings. The offensive unit was in one group, the defense in another. The special teams (for kickoffs and punts) had their own squad meeting. Everyone had to be in bed by eleven o'clock at night.

L.T. soon found out that there was a lot to learn about pro football. He had to be thinking on every play. However, he was helped and encouraged by the other Giants linebackers. He listened carefully to what they told him.

"That was a good move, Taylor," Harry Carson might say. "That was a good hit," Van Pelt would comment. "You smelled out that play," Brian Kelley would tell him.

L.T. was happy about that kind of praise. However, when he did something wrong, they told him about that, too. "You were out of position," one of the linebackers would show him. "You were fooled."

L.T. would take their advice. He realized that they had been playing pro football for years. They knew what to expect from other teams.

The sportswriters often joked with L.T. One said to him, "Do you like to watch soap operas because Harry Carson likes them?"

"I watched the soaps on TV long before I met Harry Carson." L.T. grinned.

L.T. at one of his frequent interviews.

Then they teased him because he liked to shoot a game of pool. They asked if he won a lot of money from his teammates.

"No." L.T. laughed. "I enjoy shooting pool. We just play for nickels and dimes. Pool is a good way to relax."

The Giants' coaches decided how their four linebackers would play. Brian Kelley would rush the passer. Harry Carson and Brad Van Pelt would concentrate on the running plays into the middle of the line. L.T. was "free." If he wanted to rush the passer, he could do that. Or if he thought the other team would run the ball, he did not rush the quarterback.

In college, L.T. had usually rushed the passer, and that was just what he did in the 1981 pre-season exhibition games. The Giants played four games against other teams. They sacked the quarterback seven times. L.T. got four of those sacks.

However, L.T. was not quite satisfied with himself. He said, "I have to start reading my 'keys' [assignments] better. I'm not seeing all the players the way I should."

It soon became clear that the Giants' defense would have to be outstanding. The offense seemed weak. The Giants lost the opening game of the season to the Philadelphia Eagles, but won the next game against the Washington Redskins. But the Giants' ball carriers couldn't do the job. They gained only 55 yards rushing against the Eagles and 76 yards against the Redskins.

In a game against the New Orleans Saints, L.T. found out what it was like to get hurt. He was hit from behind and knocked down. He lay on the ground for almost three minutes before he could get up. He had a pinched nerve. Yet, after a short rest, he returned to the game. The Giants won, 20–7.

After losing to Green Bay, suddenly, the Giants seemed to catch fire. They won their next three games, against the St. Louis Cardinals, the Seattle Seahawks, and the Atlanta Falcons. They felt confident that their team could make the play-offs.

But the bubble soon burst. The Giants were drubbed by the Jets. The score was 26–7. The whole offensive team played poorly.

The Giants' quarterback was sacked nine times. The receivers dropped six passes. There were several penalties for holding. The offense didn't score the touchdown; the defense did. That came about on an intercepted pass.

L.T. got two sacks that day. On one of them, he knocked down the passer for a loss of 11 yards.

Then the Giants lost again. The Green Bay Packers beat them, 26–24. Giants' coach Ray Perkins said that L.T. played his best game as a pro linebacker. L.T. seemed to be everywhere. He sacked Green Bay quarterback Lynn Dickey for a loss of 10 yards. Dickey was replaced by David Whitehurst. L.T. sacked him, too, for a loss of 8 yards. Then he forced a fumble. He broke up a pass. He made four solo tackles. He was in the Packers backfield all day long. But that wasn't good enough. The Giants had lost the game. That was what mattered most to L.T.

The Giants lost their next game. The Washington Redskins beat them, 30–27, in overtime. It was getting

L.T. studies the New York Jets' offensive line.

harder and harder to figure out the Giants. First they had won three in a row, then they lost three in a row.

The outlook was discouraging for the Giants. They had won five games and lost six so far. The next game was against the Eagles. The Eagles had a record of nine wins and only two defeats. They had beaten the Giants twelve straight times. But the Giants refused to quit.

They took on the Eagles and beat them, 20–10. The defense played a strong game. L.T. and Brad Van Pelt were outstanding. L.T. sacked the quarterback, but it didn't count. The Giants were holding and received a penalty.

But the Giants' joy did not last. They lost to the San Francisco 49ers, 17–10. The 49ers had one of the best teams in the National Football League. Yet they could score only 17 points against the Giants. Unfortunately, the Giants had very little scoring punch.

Now it seemed that the Giants were out of the play-offs. They had a record of six wins and seven losses. There were three games left to play. The Giants had to face the Los Angeles Rams, the St. Louis Cardinals, and the Dallas Cowboys. They had to win all three games to stay alive. Perhaps that was too much to ask.

The Giants hung on grimly. On a windy, cold day, they bumped heads with the Rams. And they won, 10–7. L.T. was just great. Twice he tackled a Rams' ball carrier behind the line of scrimmage for losses. He forced a fumble. On one play, L.T. came tearing into the Los Angeles' backfield. A blocker tried to stop him. L.T. pushed the blocker back. Then he reached out with one hand, grabbed the quarterback, and sacked him.

L.T. gets set to tackle the Rams' quarterback.

L.T. had developed a few tricks of his own. He laughed when he explained them to the sportswriters.

"When I'm lined up, the quarterback is looking right at me," he said. "He looks into my eyes. I wink at him. He thinks I'm going to blitz in. Sometimes I do, but sometimes I don't blitz. But the quarterback starts to worry. He loses his concentration. And that's exactly what I'm hoping for."

Onward went the Giants. They went up against the Cardinals and beat them, 20–10. L.T. was partly responsible for one touchdown. In the first quarter, he banged into Cardinal passer Neil Lomax. There was a fumble. Defensive end George Martin picked up the ball. He ran 20 yards for the score. L.T. had another sack as well.

Finally, they had to play the Dallas Cowboys. It was a tough game. At the end of four quarters the score was tied, 10–10. The teams went into overtime. The Cowboys began a drive. They tried a running play in which the quarterback pitched out to Tony Dorsett, the Cowboys' great running back. Dorsett juggled the ball for a instant. That was when L.T. jumped on his back. Dorsett dropped the ball, and L.T. recovered the fumble. The Giants went on to win, 13–10. They were in the play-offs.

It was the first time the Giants had ever been in the play-offs. In 1963 they had played the Chicago Bears for the championship of the N.F.L. There was no Super Bowl in those days. The Giants lost that championship game, 14–10.

Will L.T. blitz in? Maybe he won't—the quarterback is never sure.

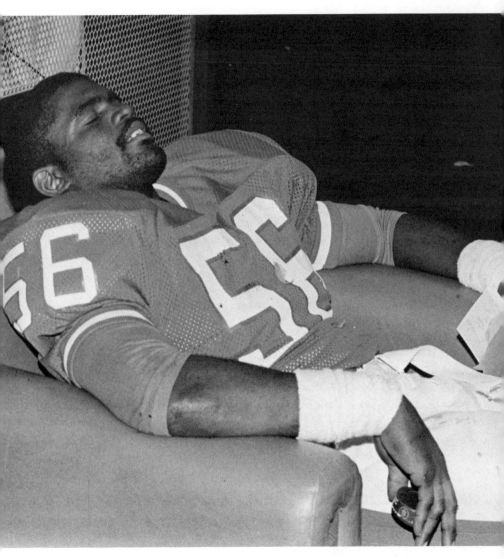

L.T. can smile when the Giants win.

In the play-offs, the first team the Giants had to face was the Philadelphia Eagles. During the season, the Giants had lost to the Eagles, then beaten them. Could they win again?

They beat the Eagles, 27–21. L.T. was in one key play. The Giants were forced to punt. When the ball came down, L.T. was waiting for the receiver. He caused a fumble. Defensive ace Beasley Reece recovered for the Giants.

Then it was on to San Francisco to play the 49ers. That was for the championship of the conference. The 49ers had a record of thirteen wins and only three losses during the regular season. The San Francisco coaches figured out a way to stop L.T. The 49ers guard, John Ayers, who was one of the best blockers in the league, was told to follow L.T. no matter where he was. Also, a tight end would help out sometimes.

L.T. managed to sack the quarterback once. He made only two solo tackles and helped out on three others. But he could not do too much more. The 49ers beat the Giants, 38–24.

The year 1981 had been a marvelous year for Lawrence Taylor. He was voted to a place on the All-League team and the All-Rookie team. He was selected to play in the Pro Bowl game.

L.T. took it easy during the spring and summer of 1982. He married his girlfriend, Linda, and bought a beautiful house in New Jersey. Since L.T. had not graduated from North Carolina, he went back to school and took a few courses.

But there were clouds looming overhead. The whole National Football League was heading for trouble.

A disappointed L.T. thinks about a game the Giants lost.

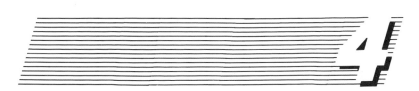

Pro football had become the most popular sport on TV. More people watched the Super Bowl than baseball's World Series. Yet football players received less money than baseball or basketball players. The players wanted more money from the owners. They wanted to share in the huge sums that the TV networks were giving the owners. The players said that they would go on strike if they did not get more money.

The players' union and the team owners tried to solve the problem. Meanwhile, the players went to summer training camp. They had to get ready for the new season.

After only one season, Lawrence Taylor had become the star of the Giants' defense. Again and again he had to prove how tough he was. In one practice, a teammate blocked him hard. He stuck his helmet into L.T.'s stomach. L.T. lay on the ground, gasping for breath.

Other teams began to zero in on L.T. He got hurt. In an exhibition game against Pittsburgh, he suffered a chip fracture of his left wrist. He hurt his left foot against the Jets. The pain was so bad that he couldn't play in the exhibition game against Miami.

L.T. was asked how he felt. He said, "This is only my second year in pro football. But my body feels like it has been twelve years."

The Giants lost the first regular game of the 1982 season to the Atlanta Falcons. The score was 16–14. The Giants were leading 14–7 late in the game. Then the Falcons scored a touchdown. The point after touchdown would tie the game. But L.T. came charging in. He jumped and raised his arms high. He blocked the kick. The score was 14–13, the Giants leading. But the Giants couldn't hold the lead. Atlanta kicked a field goal to win the game.

The next week the Giants lost to the Green Bay Packers, 27–19. L.T. played a great game. He and teammate Phil Tabor sacked quarterback Lynn Dickey for a 10-yard loss. On the next play L.T. zoomed in and threw Dickey for another 10-yard loss. But that wasn't enough to win the game.

There was no pro football the following week. The players were on strike. The team owners didn't want the strike. Neither did the players. But there seemed no way out.

L.T. said, "The players have to explain to the fans. Most folks make about $20,000 a year. Football players make a lot more. But we get knocked around a lot."

L.T. and other players continued to practice during the strike.
In this photo he is practicing pass interceptions.

Some of the Giants continued to practice during the strike. They worked out at a park in New Jersey. Once they played a game of softball at a Little League baseball field. They wanted to have some fun. Those who were right-handed batted lefty. The left-handed players batted righty. Almost every time he got to bat, L.T. smacked the ball over the fence.

Billy Ard, one of L.T.'s teammates, said, "Even if we were playing tiddledywinks, L.T. would be the best at that."

The strike lasted until November 16. Much of the football season was lost. Instead of playing sixteen games a season, in 1982 the pro football season was only nine games.

Right away, the Giants lost again. The Redskins beat them, 27–17. L.T. suffered a strained knee.

L.T. was unhappy. His knee hurt. He had lost a lot of money because of the strike. But he resolved to play his best.

After three straight losses, the Giants finally won a game. They beat the Detroit Lions, 13–6. L.T. was outstanding. He sacked the quarterback. He forced a fumble. He made three solo tackles. But his best play came when it seemed that the Lions would score a touchdown.

The score was tied, 6–6. The Lions drove down to the Giants 4-yard line. It was third down, goal to go. The Lions tried a trick play. It was a sideline pass to Horace King, a Detroit running back. L.T. saw what was going to happen. He cut in front of King and grabbed the ball on the 3-yard line. Then he raced down the sideline. The whole Detroit team was chasing him. L.T. went over the goal for the winning touchdown.

Even great players get hurt in a hard game. Here a Giants'
trainer attends to L.T.'s knee.

Taylor is lifted by teammate Terry Kinard after No. 56 intercepted a pass and ran for a touchdown.

Later, Brad Benson, a Giants' lineman, said, "There should be a law against linebackers running that fast."

It seemed that the Giants would lose their next game against the Houston Oilers. The Giants were not playing well. They were trailing 14–3. Suddenly the Giants took the lead. They scored two quick touchdowns. Now the score was 17–14 with the Giants ahead. But there was still time for Houston to come back.

The Giants' defense was just great. George Martin sacked Houston quarterback Archie Manning twice. Once the Oilers lost 2 yards. Then it was 10 yards. Finally, L.T. put the game away. He sacked the quarterback for a 15-yard loss, making the tackle with one arm.

The Giants marched on. They defeated the Philadelphia Eagles, 23–7. The Giants' defense was like a stone wall. Philadelphia did not even make one first down rushing. The Eagles' quarterback was sacked eight times. L.T. knocked down the passer three times.

Now the Giants had won three games and lost three. It was possible to make the play-offs. But that was not to be. They lost their next two games. The Redskins beat them with a field goal in the last four seconds of play. The Cardinals defeated the Giants with only twenty-seven seconds left to play. The Giants finished the season by beating the Eagles again, 26–24.

Once again L.T. was named to the All-Pro team. He was also voted the top linebacker in the league.

At the end of the season, head coach Ray Perkins left the team to become a college football coach. He was replaced by Bill Parcells, who had been an assistant coach with the Giants.

Redskins' fullback John Riggins and L.T. congratulate each other after a tough game.

L.T. with new head coach Bill Parcells in training camp.

L.T. had played pro football for two years. Everybody said he was the best linebacker. But other rookies coming out of college were getting more money than L.T. Now he understood why Carson, Van Pelt, and Kelley had been so unhappy. They had proved how good they were. They had played for years. Yet L.T. got more money, even though he had not yet played a single minute of pro football.

L.T. told the Giants he wanted his contract changed. He said if he didn't get a raise, he would not play in 1983. The Giants said L.T. had to play. He had signed a contract.

L.T. was not with the Giants for a while. He was in the stands, watching, when the team played exhibition games. The Giants knew he was needed and told L.T. to report to the team. They promised to talk about a new contract after the season was over. L.T. agreed to come back.

The Giants' had a terrible season in 1983. They won only three games, lost twelve, and tied one.

The Giants offense was bad. Often the team would drive down the field and would get close to the goal line. Then a running back would fumble. The quarterback would get sacked. The other team would intercept a pass. Something always went wrong.

But the defense continued to shine. L.T. was always in the thick of things. He had learned a great deal about the game. For instance, in college he did not have to cover a pass receiver. In the pros, that was part of his job. L.T. made a few mistakes at first. But he soon learned how to play against a receiver.

Somehow, L.T. often knew what the opposing team was going to do. In a game against the Seattle Seahawks, L.T. seemed to be all over the field. The Giants lost that game, but L.T. covered himself with glory. On one play he tackled star running back Curt Warner for a 2-yard loss. Then the Seahawks tried a deep reverse. The quarterback handed the ball to a halfback, who began to run around end. Suddenly the halfback gave the ball to another Seahawk. He ran in the opposite direction. L.T. wasn't fooled for a minute. He chased the man with the football. He tackled him for a 13-yard loss.

In spite of the Giants' poor season, L.T. was chosen to play in the Pro Bowl game. So was his buddy, Harry Carson.

Now L.T. wanted the Giants to keep the promise made to him. A new contract would pay him millions of dollars, but sometimes contracts are difficult to work out. They take time. L.T. became very impatient. He began talking to a man named Donald Trump, who owned the New Jersey Generals. That was a team in the United States Football League.

For a while there was much confusion. Even if he did not get more money, L.T. was still under contract to the Giants. Some newspapers said L.T. did sign to play with the Generals. Others said he would play for the Giants.

In the end L.T. stayed with the Giants. Now at last he had become a millionaire. And he was eager for the 1984 season to begin. He was determined that the Giants would make the play-offs again.

The millionaire Lawrence Taylor. He always wears sharp clothes.

By 1984, Brad Van Pelt and Brian Kelley were no longer with the Giants. They were replaced by two young players, Byron Hunt and Andy Headen. The new linebackers were good players, but Lawrence Taylor and Harry Carson were outstanding, as usual.

The Giants opened the season by defeating Philadelphia, 28–27. L.T. played a nice game. But he was only warming up for the game against the Dallas Cowboys.

The Giants creamed the Cowboys, 28–7. L.T. was like a wild man. In the second period he sacked quarterback Gary Hogeboom twice. In the third period, the Cowboys had the ball on the Giants 6-yard line. L.T. blitzed in. He cracked into the passer. There was a fumble. Linebacker Andy Headen picked up the loose football and ran 81 yards for a touchdown.

Almost always the Giants play great defensive football. Here
L.T. listens to advice from defensive coach Bill Belichick.

Just seven minutes later, there was L.T. again. Once more he sacked the quarterback. There was another fumble. The Giants recovered.

After the game, Gary Hogeboom said, "We were trying for short passes. It's a play where the quarterback counts, 1—2—3. Then he throws the ball. Taylor had me when I reached the count of 2. It's supposed to be a quick pass. Lawrence Taylor was quicker."

Lawrence Taylor was the best linebacker in pro football. Everybody said so. Also, he had a beautiful wife and a fine young son he called "T.J."—Taylor Junior. He had plenty of money. He had a nice house in New Jersey. Everybody was praising him. But very few fans knew he had a problem. It was alcohol.

Even in college, L.T. had gone to a bar once in a while. He had a few beers. The beers never bothered him. He was always in condition to play. But now he had begun to drink hard liquor.

Perhaps the drinking began in 1983 when the Giants had the terrible season. L.T. hated to lose. After a bad game he would sit by his locker muttering to himself. Then he would get dressed and go somewhere to have some drinks. It wasn't beer; it was liquor. He seemed to be trying to forget all the lost games.

In 1984, when the Giants began winning, L.T. kept on drinking liquor. He could handle it at first. It did not seem to interfere with the way he played football. When he went into a bar, everybody slapped him on the back. They told him how great he was. They wanted to buy him a drink. L.T. was very friendly, especially when the Giants won. He accepted the drinks.

When the Giants lost to the Redskins, it was not the defense's fault. The offense was awful. The pass receivers dropped the ball five times. The Redskins scored two touchdowns because the Giants fumbled. The 'Skins intercepted three passes. They sacked the Giants quarterback five times.

L.T. was the star of the game against Tampa Bay. He forced a fumble, and Jim Burt fell on the ball. The Giants scored three plays later. Then he blitzed in on quarterback Steve DeBerg. The passer had to get rid of the ball in a hurry. It was a bad throw. Andy Headen intercepted. After the game, Harry Carson said, "L.T. is quick, he's fast, he's strong, he's fearless. Sometimes I think he's Superman."

Yet, sometimes even the Giants' defense did not play well. The San Francisco 49ers beat them, 49–10. And L.T. said, "I'm *not* Superman. I'm just a good player."

L.T. was never jealous of his teammates, particularly the linebackers, and the Giants always seemed to have good ones. Carl Banks and Gary Reasons helped the Giants beat the Atlanta Falcons, 19–7. L.T. said, "I'm proud of them. It's good when young guys like that can step in and play so well. And they're just rookies."

But even the Giants' defense could slip. When the Eagles won, it was because of bad tackling. Then the Giants made up for that by beating the Redskins. Everybody played well in that game. And, against the Cowboys, L.T. and Leonard Marshall sacked quarterback Danny White five times. Once, L.T. hit White so hard that he had to leave the game.

Taylor forces Tampa Bay quarterback Steve DeBerg to throw the ball before he was ready. It was a bad pass. Andy Headen of the Giants intercepted.

L.T. lowers the boom on Dallas quarterback Danny White.

The Giants finished the 1984 season with a record of nine victories and seven defeats and made it into the play-offs.

The Los Angeles Rams and the Giants faced each other. It was a rugged game. The defense was absolutely great. In the fourth quarter, the Giants put on a goal-line stand and stopped a touchdown. L.T. forced a fumble twice. He and teammate George Martin banged into quarterback Jeff Kemp and forced a fumble again. Andy Headen recovered for the Giants. They won, 16–13, but it was close all the way.

The San Francisco 49ers beat the Giants for the conference championship. The score was 21–10. The defense was good, but the Giants couldn't score many points.

Once again Lawrence Taylor was named to the All-Pro squad. It was the fourth year in a row he had made the team. Yet some sportswriters said that L.T. had not played as well as usual that season. There were games when he wasn't sharp at all.

But, at the start of the 1985 season, L.T. looked like his old self again. The Giants shut out the Eagles in the opening game, 21–0. L.T. and his teammate, right end Leonard Marshall, were outstanding. They sacked the quarterback five times. L.T. was putting pressure on the passer almost every play.

Then the Packers beat the Giants, 23–20. L.T. seemed tired. There were rumors about the reason he played poorly. Reporters said he had been in a bar until past midnight.

L.T. had changed. He had trouble keeping his temper. The second time the Giants played the Eagles, the New York team won again, 16–10. L.T. sacked the quarterback hard, and a penalty flag was thrown. But it was a mistake. There was no penalty. The flag was picked up again, but L.T. did not see the official pick up the flag. He was so angry that he threw his helmet to the ground. He was penalized 15 yards for unsportsmanlike conduct.

In his next two games, L.T. played badly. He had no zip in his tackles. The Giants lost both those games. The Cowboys won, 30–29, and then the Cincinnati Bengals beat the Giants, 35–30. That was L.T.'s worst game of the season. Even John Madden, who broadcast the games on TV, said so.

L.T. seemed to know he was letting his team down. When the Giants played the Redskins, he was terrific. He sacked the quarterback twice. He made thirteen solo tackles.

After the game, sportswriters asked why he had played well.

L.T. said, "I went back to the old stuff. I prepared myself. I got to sleep on time. I didn't go to the bars as much."

But it didn't last. L.T. couldn't seem to get going. Although the Giants won three games in a row, L.T. didn't help very much. He refused to talk to sportswriters.

When the Giants played the Redskins again, they lost, 23–21. L.T. and Gary Reasons crashed through the line and smashed into quarterback Joe Theismann. They

A familiar scene. Taylor and George Martin slap hands after
sacking the quarterback.

hit him so hard that he suffered a fractured leg. L.T. knew in a second how badly the Redskins' passer was hurt. He got up quickly. He called to the Redskins' bench to bring out a stretcher. L.T. was truly sorry about that.

L.T. was trying hard to return to his old form. He played a great game against St. Louis. He sacked quarterback Neil Lomax hard. Lomax had to leave the game.

It was an up-and-down season for L.T. He did not play well against the Cleveland Browns, but he snapped back in a game against the Houston Oilers. It was win one, lose one. The Cowboys beat the Giants. The Giants beat the Steelers.

L.T. and his team had made the play-offs again. They finished the season with ten wins and six losses.

In 1984, the Giants had faced the 49ers in the play-offs. Now they were facing them again. This time the story was different. The Giants won, 17–3, but the 49ers did not play their usual good game. Some of the San Francisco players were hurt, and their receivers dropped ten passes. Still, L.T. and the defense played a fine game.

Next they faced the Chicago Bears in the semifinals for the conference championship. With only one loss all season and their defense the best in pro football, the Bears were the best team in the whole league. They were favored to win.

It was a cold day when the Bears and Giants clashed. A fierce wind was blowing. The Bears' defense was outstanding, but the Giants' defense was also great. The

L.T. chasing down Washington Redskins' quarterback Joe Theismann.

score was 0–0, and the Giants were deep in their own territory. It was fourth down. The Giants had to punt. But the Giants' kicker missed the ball completely. Perhaps the wind just blew the ball away from his toe. The ball fell to the ground. A Chicago player picked up the ball and ran into the end zone for a touchdown. The Bears led, 7–0.

The Bears did not seem to fear L.T. In the first half, they ran right at him. In the second half of the game they ran to the other side of the line. The Bears blocked L.T. most of the game. Even the Bears' quarterback, Jim McMahon, blocked him out of one play. L.T. looked angry when that happened.

Matt Suhey, the Bears' fullback, also blocked L.T. Suhey crouched down. He threw his body across L.T.'s legs.

"You're a baby," L.T. yelled to Suhey. "Stand up and block me like a man."

Suhey wouldn't do that. The way he blocked L.T. was perfectly legal. Later, Suhey said, "Taylor has so much speed. He has so much power. That was the only way I could block him."

By the end of the game all the Bears were calling L.T. names. Jim Burt, the Giants' lineman, spoke to Jay Hilgenberg, the Bears' center. Burt said, "Just forget about it. That's the way L.T. is."

The Giants lost that game, 21–0. The Giants' defense was good. The Bears' defense was better.

After the game L.T. sat in the locker room. He was scowling. He said to reporters, "Don't even come near me."

L.T. did not have a good season in 1985. Sportswriters had been saying all year that something was wrong with him. But he was picked to play in the Pro Bowl again. Some reporters said he didn't deserve to be picked. That was not the truth. He was really the star of the Giants' defense.

In 1985, L.T. had led the Giants in tackles. He had 83 solo tackles and 21 assists. He led the Giants in forced fumbles. He had four. He was tied with Jim Burt in recovering fumbles. Each had two. He was second in sacking the quarterback. Leonard Marshall had 15½, L.T. had 13½.

L.T. had played pro football five years. He had been named top linebacker in the league by the Players Association. He won that award four times. Twice he was named Most Valuable Defensive Player by the Associated Press. He was voted the Defensive Player of the Year.

Yet he was not the same old Lawrence Taylor anymore. Something was wrong. Lawrence Taylor knew that, too.

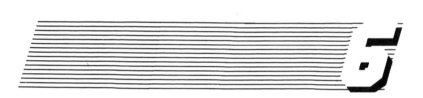

The date was Friday, February 14, 1986. Howard Cosell, the famous sports reporter, began his radio broadcast. His voice was sad.

Cosell said that Lawrence Taylor was in a drug rehabilitation clinic. No one had told him to go there. L.T. had made his own decision. He had a drug problem. He was a sick man.

L.T.'s mother said she was shocked at the news. "I have nothing to say about it," said Giants' coach Bill Parcells. Officials in the National Football League said they didn't know anything about it.

Was it still alcohol? Or was it cocaine? Was it both alcohol and cocaine? Nobody seemed to be sure.

"I heard he drank a lot," said Ali Haji-Sheikh, the Giants' placekicker. "I hope he gets straightened out."

Leonard Marshall said, "I'd be surprised if it was cocaine. Everybody knew he had other problems."

Harry Carson hardly spoke at all. He merely said, "Nothing really surprises me. Things just happen, that's how it is."

All the players were sorry for L.T., but they were sure he would come out all right. One player, who had had a drug problem, said he was certain L.T. would be cured.

"Taylor is a very strong man," the player said. "He's a better man than I was. I didn't know I had a drug problem. I thought I could handle the stuff. But I couldn't. Taylor found out by himself. I was cured. Taylor will be cured too."

When L.T. left the clinic, he would not talk to reporters. He was not rude to anyone; he simply did not want to talk about what had happened to him. He asked the reporters to understand what he had done.

For most of the spring of 1986 L.T. played a lot of golf with friends. He played in charity tournaments. But he would not give interviews.

Toward the end of May 1986, the Giants had a mini-camp for five days. L.T. still would not talk to reporters, but Giants' coach Bill Parcells did.

"I don't expect Taylor to say anything," Parcells said. "He has asked for your cooperation, but I don't think he expects it. He doesn't trust you guys. If I were Taylor I would do the same thing. In fact, I would advise him not to talk to you."

Then Parcells added, "I hope things work out."

All sports fans were rooting for Lawrence Taylor to make a comeback. Once he was the best linebacker in pro football. He could be the greatest again.

The Giants were favored to win their division in 1986, but the team got off to a bad start. Dallas beat them, 31-28, in the last 76 seconds of play. But the Giants rallied and won their next five games.

Lawrence Taylor also started slowly. In the first four games he had only one and a half sacks. But the entire "front seven"—the three linemen and four linebackers—were improving with every game. No team could run with the ball against that defense. The Giants went swarming in to stop the ball carriers. They blitzed in on the quarterbacks, gang-tackled the runners, and knocked down passes.

Most of the time L.T. went charging in. Even when he was stopped, that didn't mean he was out of the play. In a game against St. Louis, Taylor was knocked to the ground. But he got up and sacked quarterback Neil Lomax for a loss of 11 yards. He was double-teamed often, but that meant other Giants linebackers were left open. Carl Banks, the other outside linebacker, was almost as good as Taylor at stopping the run or defending against short passes.

The Giants' opponents began to zero in on Taylor. L.T. would shift from one side of the line to the other. One time, Taylor changed his position and lined up against Ray Brown, a rookie guard. Brown was so startled he stood up from his three-point stance. That was illegal movement and cost his team a five-yard penalty.

The Giants lost to Seattle, but that was not the defense's fault. The score was 17-12. Giants' quarterback Phil Simms was sacked seven times. The Giants allowed only 56 yards rushing by the Seahawks great runner, Curt Warner.

On and on went the Giants. They beat the Redskins, the Cowboys, the Eagles, the Vikings, the Broncos, and the 49ers. Then, in a showdown for first place in their division, the Giants beat the Redskins again, 24-14. Lawrence Taylor was a wild man on the field. He sacked the quarterback three times, forced a fumble, and made two tackles. The marvelous defense made six interceptions.

The Giants closed out the season with a record of fourteen victories and only two losses. Lawrence Taylor won a great many awards. His twenty and a half sacks were tops in the NFL. He was voted Most Valuable Player in the league. He was named to the All Pro team for the sixth time in a row and was voted Player of the Year by the Associated Press.

The Giants went all the way. They blasted the 49ers and the Redskins in the playoff games, and crushed the Broncos in the Super Bowl game, 39-20.

Lawrence Taylor had made a magnificent comeback. But he gave much of the credit to coach Bill Parcells. Accepting the MVP award, L.T. said, "This award should have my name and Bill Parcells' name on it. I thank him for giving me the strength necessary to win it."

Lawrence Taylor made mistakes. He admits that. But with the help of his good friends he became once again the finest player in the National Football League.

INDEX